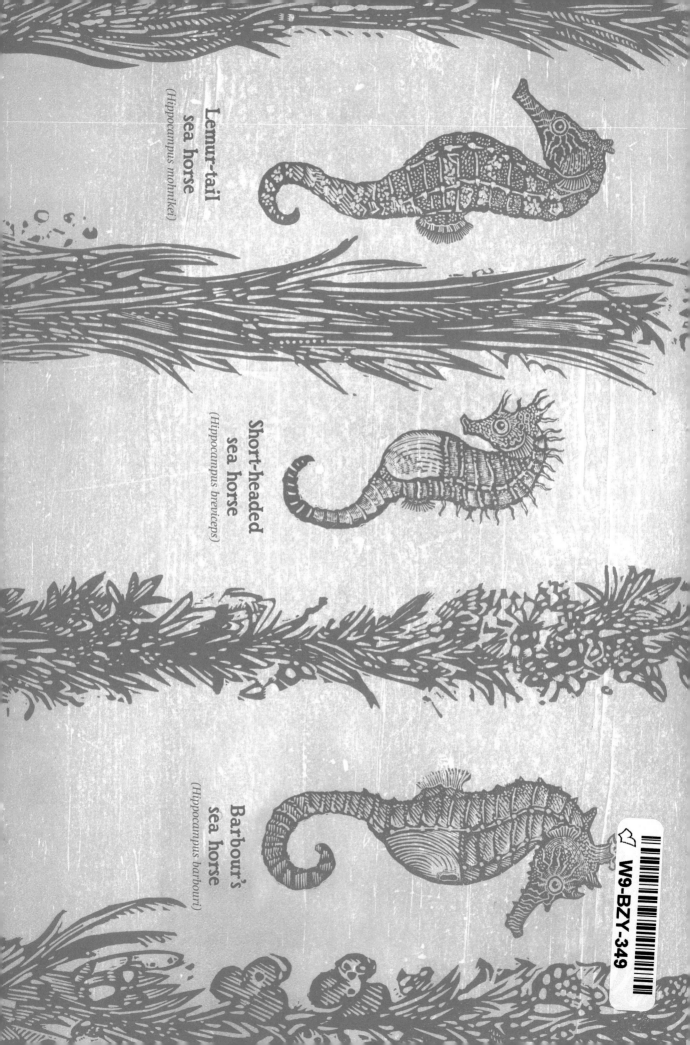

Lemur-tail
sea horse
(*Hippocampus mohnikei*)

Short-headed
sea horse
(*Hippocampus breviceps*)

Barbour's
sea horse
(*Hippocampus barbouri*)

For Margaret
C. B.

For Dominic
J. L.

The author, illustrator, and publisher would like to thank Colin Wells
of the National Marine Aquarium in Plymouth, England, for his expert
advice and guidance during the preparation of this book.

Text copyright © 2006 by Chris Butterworth
Illustrations copyright © 2006 by John Lawrence

First U. S. edition 2006

Library of Congress Cataloging-in-Publication Data is available.

Library of Congress Catalog Card Number 2005050755

ISBN 0-7636-2989-8

10 9 8 7 6 5 4 3 2 1

Printed in China

This book was typeset in Lawrence.
The illustrations were made from vinyl engravings,
watercolor washes, and printed wood textures.

Candlewick Press
2067 Massachusetts Avenue
Cambridge, Massachusetts 02140

visit us at www.candlewick.com

SEA HORSE

The Shyest Fish in the Sea

Chris Butterworth

illustrated by

John Lawrence

CANDLEWICK PRESS
CAMBRIDGE, MASSACHUSETTS

In the warm ocean,
among the waving sea-grass meadows,
an eye like a small black bead
is watching the fish dart by.
Who does it belong to?

SEA HORSE—
one of the shyest fish in the sea.

7

Sea Horse has a head like a horse,
a tail like a monkey,
and a pouch like a kangaroo.
This one is a Barbour's sea horse.
He has tiny prickles down
his back, like a dragon.
He may not look much like a fish . . .
but that's what he is.

For a long time, no one was sure what kind of animal the sea horse was.
Its scientific name is Hippocampus, which means "horselike sea monster."

Sea Horse
swims upright.
He moves himself
through the water
with the little fins
on his head
and the larger one
on his back.

He can only swim slowly,
so if a hungry snapper cruises by,
    looking for a snack,
Sea Horse does something very clever:
he holds still and changes color
    (now you see him . . .)
until he's almost invisible
    (now you don't!).

The way sea horses change the color of their skin

to blend in with their surroundings

is called camouflage.

Sea horses have
hard bony ridges
all down their bodies.
Not many other
creatures eat sea
horses—probably
because they're
just too difficult
to swallow.

Every day at sunrise, Sea Horse swims slowly off to meet his mate. They twist their tails together and twirl gently around, changing color until they match.

Sea horses are faithful to one mate and often pair up for life.

Today Sea Horse's mate is full of ripe eggs.
The two of them dance till sunset,
and then she puts her eggs into his pouch.

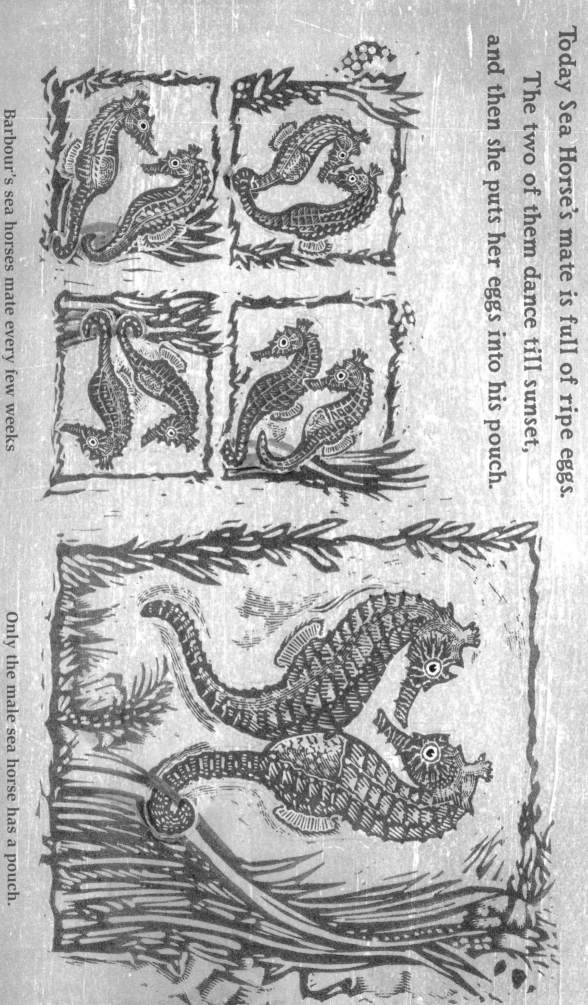

Barbour's sea horses mate every few weeks
during the breeding season.

Only the male sea horse has a pouch.
Only the female sea horse can grow eggs.

Sea horses are the only
male fish to get "pregnant"
like this, growing their young
inside their own bodies.

Sea Horse sways about
to get the eggs settled in,
then seals his pouch shut tight.

Safe inside, the dots in the eggs begin to grow into baby sea horses. They break out of their eggs and keep on growing, every one with a head like a tiny horse and a tail like a tiny monkey.

A few weeks later,
Sea Horse finds a quiet place
to hide among the corals.
It's time for the babies to be born.
He works hard all day
and through the night,
bending, squeezing, and pushing,
shooting hundreds
of babies out of his pouch. . . .

Barbour's sea horses can have two to three hundred babies at one time.

17

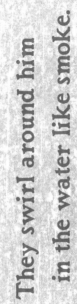

They swirl around him
in the water like smoke.

One or two of the babies hang on to Dad's nose
for a while (it's the first and biggest thing
they've seen), but when they let go . . . .

Each tiny new sea horse is a perfect copy of its parents and is ready for life on its own as soon as it's born.

they are so tiny and light that the current soon floats them away.

Sea horses live on plankton——

This new sea horse is only
as long as your eyelash,
but she can find
her own food right away.
Her eyes move separately
from each other
(one can peer up
while the other looks down),
so she can spot food
coming from any direction.

tiny creatures that float along with the current.

With one quick slurp, she sucks
her catch into the end of her snout
and swallows it whole—
sea horses don't have teeth.

When she is big enough,
Sea Horse curls up her tail
and sinks to the seabed.

To drop lower
in the water,
sea horses
tuck in
their necks
and roll up
their tails.

To rise higher,
they uncurl
themselves
till they
are almost
as straight
as pencils.

Sea horses cannot live where the currents are very strong. They would be swept away.

She is safer here. Her camouflage protects her, and if a storm scoops the sea into huge waves or passing boats send currents sweeping by, there are plenty of things to hang on to.

Sea horses have prehensile tails, which means they can grasp things tightly with them.

When she is even bigger, Sea Horse picks one patch of reef as her home. She wraps her tail around a coral branch. This is her holdfast. . . . Wherever she goes, she'll keep coming back to this holdfast.

Male Barbour's sea horses range over only a few square yards. The females' range is twice as big, or even bigger.

In a few months,

this little sea horse

will be ready to mate.

She'll spend the rest of her life

on the reef, watching for food,

meeting her mate, and trying

to stay almost invisible. . . .

Barbour's sea horses can mate by the age of six months and are fully grown at about a year.

Who's that peering
from the coral?

Shhh, she's a sea horse.

Index

Look up the pages to find out about all these sea horse things.

Don't forget to look at both kinds of words — **this kind** and this kind.

About Sea Horses

The sea horses in this book are Barbour's sea horses; you can see other kinds of sea horses on the pages at either end of the book. Marine zoologists think there are 35 sea horse species, but they may still find others. Many kinds of sea horses need protecting — millions die each year when they are taken from the seas to be sold and when humans disturb the quiet waters where they live.

About the Author

Chris Butterworth loves the sea and the amazing things that live in it. "A sea horse looks as magical as a mermaid," she says, "but while mermaids are made up, sea horses really exist. We need to know as much about them as we can, so we can protect them better. Otherwise, one day sea horses might join the mermaids and exist only in stories."

About the Illustrator

John Lawrence was born by the sea and has always loved swimming and puttering along the shore. "I had never met any sea horses," he says, "so this book has given me the opportunity I missed. They are really exciting to draw, and I have tried to imagine how it must be to live under the water like them."

Pygmy
sea horse
(Hippocampus bargibanti)

Pacific
sea horse
(Hippocampus ingens)